W9-BEU-656

FOOD FOR BODY AND SOUL

Recipes For Recovery

COLLECTED AND EDITED BY
Gina Ogden, Ph.D.

Health Communications, Inc.
Deerfield Beach, Florida

Gina Ogden, Ph.D.
Cambridge, Massachusetts

Library of Congress Cataloging-in-Publication Data

Food for body and soul: recovery tips and tidbits / collected and edited by Gina Ogden.

    p.   cm.
    ISBN 1-55874-159-3
    1. Mental health — Nutritional aspects. 2. Co-dependence (Psychology). I. Ogden, Gina.
    RC455.4.N8F66   1991   91-27024
    641.5′63—dc20   CIP

©1991 Gina Ogden
ISBN 1-55874-159-3

Publisher: Health Communications, Inc.
          3201 S.W. 15th Street
          Deerfield Beach, Florida 33442-8190

For Lainey
my sister, through thick and thin

Food For Body And Soul is also dedicated to people who do not have enough to eat. Ten percent of the author's and agent's proceeds will be donated to the City of Cambridge for projects to feed women and children.

You should never eat in one sitting
any more than you can lift.

— Miss Piggy

Acknowledgments

This book is a Stone Soup, flavored by all of its contributors:

The staff at Health Communications, especially Marie Stilkind, Reta Thomas, Peter Vegso, Gary Seidler, Teri Miller, Lisa Moro, Randy McKenzie and Diane Glynn.

Barbara Haber, who welcomed me into the cookbook world.

Peggy Clark, who introduced me to M.F.K. Fisher.

Sheila Shaw, who named me Lady Potluck.

Debra Cash, Bernardine Hayes, Jane Redmont and Ellen Stone, my groupies, who encouraged and fed me, body and soul.

And of course the authors, whose recipes make *Food For Body And Soul* a true potluck.

Contents

RUMINATIONS FROM THE INNER KITCHEN

COMFORT FOODS

AFFIRMATIVE SALADS AND APPETIZERS

MAIN DISHES FOR LIGHTNESS OF BEING

CELEBRATORY INDULGENCES

FOOD FOR AFTERTHOUGHT

Foreword

In reading through the recipes and commentaries in *Food for Body and Soul*, I am reminded that food can be a powerful symbol for life's most positive impulses and experiences, like nurturance, healing, spirituality and celebration. As the various contributors make clear, food connects us with moments from the past and explains why some people take comfort from such nursery fare as bowls of oatmeal, mashed potatoes or perhaps a cup of hot cocoa accompanied by cinnamon toast. These are simple foods associated with childhood, a time which should, if we are lucky, represent innocence and well-being.

But sometimes, as adults, we must create our own symbols and our own rituals in order to construct a consciousness of well-being. Traditional holidays cannot be relied upon to recall cherished memories, so perhaps we should invent our own. It seems to me that cooking, and particularly the sharing of good food, lends itself to this goal. For example, I have a friend who invites me to an annual winter solstice party. On the longest night of the year, an established group of friends gather in her cheerful home, first to dine, then to share our personal summaries of the past year. Some years we are asked to bring a poem or some other reading, other years we just speak spontaneously, but not before we have been amply fed with warm food.

I know a couple who are famous for their much anticipated "bread and soup" parties, which take place whenever a visiting friend comes to town. The hosts make the soup and guests bring bread or perhaps a salad or dessert. The parties always turn out well, with enough food in enough variety for all who may turn up. Such rituals are comforting to friends and not a burden on hosts. Whether or not you think of yourself as an experienced cook or party-giver, you can still bring people together on some happy occasion in order to break bread.

Parties in honor of friends who are either going away or coming back from some extended trip are always deeply appreciated. Or you might consider a party in honor of yourself for having completed some onerous task like cleaning out the basement or garage. At the moment I am thinking about having a party for myself to celebrate my finally getting rid of a bad permanent. The menu, I think, will be a salad of curly endive and fiddle-head ferns, with a spiral-shaped pasta for the entrée, and a dessert of frozen yogurt decorated with chocolate curls.

You get the idea! Let food be the center of some joyous occasion for you, and let it be fun.

Barbara Haber

Barbara Haber is the curator of books at the Schlesinger Library, Radcliffe College, Cambridge, Massachusetts. She has written and edited books and articles related to women's history. The Schlesinger Library has recently organized the Radcliffe Culinary Friends group with membership open to the public.

Food For Body And Soul

The year I turned six, the bombs dropped on Pearl Harbor and my hard-luck, hard-drinking family split apart at the seams like a two-dollar suit. My father and brother left home to become war heroes, and my sister was farmed out to a live-in school in the country. Doomed to grow up in a cold house alone with a mother who couldn't get out of bed in the morning, I added my own devilish twist to the situation by staging a sit-down strike at the dinner table. I refused to eat.

That marked the beginning of my consciousness of food and was the only — mercifully brief — time in my life I can remember not being energized by the thought of eating something. I love how food smells and looks and tastes, and in adulthood I happily seek rituals around it to supply the feelings of warmth and fullness I missed out on as a child.

I sometimes imagine I could map my life by conjuring forth the foods I was eating or thinking about eating at various times and places.

I might start with a Brownie snapshot taken just about the time of my sit-down strike. I am holding my grandmother's hand. She lived in faraway Middletown, Ohio, and I only ever got to be with her a few times before she died. We are standing in front of a bakery and I am looking not at Grandma but at a sign that spells out *PASTRIES ARE THE ANSWER.*

My childhood and teens were the chocolate years, punctuated by Bolster bars and pre-packaged Devil Dogs gulped while walking along on the street, hoping I didn't meet my English teacher or whoever was my worshiped idol of the moment.

But when I think of beginning to nurture body and soul, I think of the cups of tea consumed during the three years I spent in London in the early '60s. English winters are damp and long and I was too poor to afford heat, but tea was cheap. I bought it pungent and black from the tea merchant down the road, who measured it in quarter-pound twists from giant casks with labels from India and China.

The ritual of warming the pot was something I learned from Odette, a poet friend who made the grey afternoons bearable by fixing me tea on an electric hotplate in her rented room with cabbage rose wallpaper. She had an earthenware teapot, comfortably brown, like

3

a house sparrow. She heated water to a rolling boil and filled the pot right up to the top. For a minute or two we would cup our palms around it until color began to rise in our cheeks. Then she emptied out the water, added a couple of fistsful of tea leaves and filled the pot up again with more boiling water. Finally she swaddled the pot in an Irish linen tea towel to keep the heat in and let it sit while she toasted crumpets to eat with sweet Devon butter and strawberry jam.

In those days cholesterol, caffeine and sugar had not been identified as health hazards, and so this ritual of strong tea and crumpets slathered with jam and butter was undertaken as a life-affirming one.

Today when I need something to keep me from dropping off in the afternoon, I retain the spirit of this ritual but in a more health-conscious way. I use herb tea because my system can no longer tolerate the jolt from caffeine.

I have been known to grow patches of spearmint, peppermint and lemon balm on the south side of the house, harvest bunches of them during the summer and hang them upside down in paper bags to dry. A few heaping tablespoons of these, dried, crumbled and prepared like Odette's English tea, can make a Massachusetts winter afternoon worth living. To make it easier on yourself you can use tea bags — a well-stocked health food store will give you a pick of about 37 different flavors.

Instead of crumpets dripping with butter and jam, you can munch out on organic rice cakes. If you need something soft and squishy to go along with the crunch, spread the rice cakes with almond butter . . . also from the health food store. Voila! A combination that makes a complete protein and helps you feel virtuous all at the same time. Food for the body, food for the soul.

When I close my eyes and think what I would like to eat right now, I think of the flan made famous by my friend Peggy — a *crème caramel* she brings to potluck dinners, and one year gave as holiday gifts in white ceramic bowls she wrapped in brightly colored foil. One spring afternoon, in a pinch for time, we carried leftover flan to the Boston

Marathon and sucked it out of plastic bags like winos.

Here is Peggy's recipe for flan. She says she's moving on to other things in her kitchen, so she insists that this is her Flan Song. Certainly it's enough to make you sing, and maybe even do a little dance.

Peggy's Flan Song

Peggy tells me this is a dead ripoff from the *Joy of Cooking*, except that she's invented an easy way to make the *caramel*:

Start by putting 1 tablespoonful of sugar in each of several custard cups, and bake in a 350° oven for about 15 minutes until the sugar caramelizes itself.

Then beat together in a bowl:

4 egg yolks
2 cups milk
2 tablespoons sugar
A pinch salt
1 teaspoon vanilla

Pour this not-too-foaming mixture into the slightly cooled custard cups. Set the filled cups in a flattish pan full of water and put them back in the 350°

oven for about an hour, until a knife stuck into the middle of each flan comes out clean.

When the flans are cool, turn them upside down onto a plate where they will shimmy slightly as the sweet brown juices run down their creamy sides.

With great care and a delicate sense of balance, Peggy says flan can be eaten in bed. She adds that statistics prove that people who eat flan once a week live long contented lives.

Is Peggy's flan a miracle food that synthesizes health and pleasure? Alas, not entirely. The fact is, it is full of milk and sugar, which I have come to understand the hard way can be poison for adult children of alcoholics, like myself, who are subject to mood swings and who have developed arthritic knees. In food, as in all things, there are choices to make, and each one of us may have different needs at different ages and stages.

I have tried substituting honey for the sugar in Peggy's recipe, though there is no substitute for the milk. Lactose intolerance is a condition many adults develop. If you want to find out if you have it, try cutting out all (I mean *all*) dairy products for a month and see if you breathe more freely, get rid of headaches or nagging colds, think more clearly and enjoy improved digestion.

Sugar is a drug. It's addictive, it's a mood alterer and it also plays havoc with your immune system by killing off your white blood cells. Its use has been linked to both schizophrenia and cancer. I have a friend who has labeled her sugar jar "White Death," although she continues to use sugar because she loves the taste.

When I was diagnosed with raging rheumatoid arthritis in 1980, I began to understand that what I ate affected my health. It was rather late in life to learn this basic lesson but, with the wisdom of hindsight, I figure late is better than never.

Medical doctors could not cure what I had, and anti-inflammatory pills only made me sicker. If it had not been for my friend Anne, I shudder to think what shape I would be in today.

Anne brought me to her house and showed me that food for body and soul can sometimes mean a radical change from old expected rituals. She supervised a ten-day vegetable juice fast and taught me to extract brightly colored, mineral-rich concoctions from carrots, celery, parsley and beets. I sipped these at two-hour intervals and felt calm and energized, nurtured and amazingly filled as my pain and swelling magically disappeared.

With this turning point in food consciousness, I knew I had consumed my last Bolster bar and tossed back my last glass of wine. I had never been addicted to alcohol (only to alcoholics) but after cleaning out my system by fasting, I could no longer drink more than a teaspoonful without experiencing scary heart palpitations. I also became an overnight vegetarian because meat had ceased to taste like food.

I discovered the ritual pleasures of food for health. I kept a garden and ate out of it, plucking huge salads of spinach, radishes and young chard leaves to toss with olive oil and basil vinegar. You can make your own herb vinegars by loosely packing a jar with fresh basil or tarragon or whatever you like most, then filling it up with cider vinegar and letting it sit for a few weeks in your cupboard. Some years I bottle this in wine bottles begged from friends and give it away at Christmas.

My recipe for dealing with too many tomatoes at the end of the growing

season: Keep It Simple. Wash however many you're willing to cope with, cut them up in small pieces, toss them into pint containers, stick them in the freezer and forget about them until winter.

Then, when you are yearning for a shot of pure health, saute an onion the size of your fist in a little olive oil until it turns translucent, empty two pint containers of the frozen tomatoes into the pan, cover, turn the heat down low and wait.

In half an hour you will have a nourishing, heartwarming soup that brings summer to your soul. Even the smell is healing. It tastes even better the next day — if you can hold off that long. My daughter Cathy likes to add ginger and peppercorns and cilantro, so that when you eat it your nose runs and tears stream down your cheeks. This can be extremely therapeutic if you are trying to beat the flu.

One of my life's recent gifts is that my daughter has grown up and has begun her own rituals of nurturing me — often with food. When I go to visit her in St. Paul, she bakes me a special health bread, which we eat with soup. Or sometimes she serves herb tea brewed in a teapot, properly warmed, as I learned from Odette in long-ago London. And then we talk and talk and talk.

Cathy's bread is never quite the same twice, but it always tastes just right.

Cathy's Bread For Mom

Sprinkle 2 scant tablespoons of yeast in 1 cup of warm water. Mix in ¼ cup honey or molasses — honey for lightness, molasses for the iron — and let the mixture sit to foam.

Meanwhile, mix any combo of the following dry ingredients until you have 6 cups:

Whole wheat flour
White flour
Soy flour
Rye flour (for heartier taste)

Rolled oats (for sweeter taste) — this is fun, Cathy says, because you make it like oatmeal with the butter and hot water listed below and mix it up all warm.

Dried fruits or herbs

A handful of sunflower and sesame seeds

½ cup dry milk

2 tablespoons wheat germ

Add about 2 cups of warm liquid: This can be water or soup stock. Cathy says if she's feeling particularly daring, she'll use leftover soup, like bean and spinach soup, mashed up. This makes a very powerful bread to eat with hummus (see page 41).

Add the yeast mixture and 2 tablespoons of oil or butter.

Let it all sit in a bowl until it gains a sense of itself. Then turn it out onto a floured board. Flour your hands up, take off your wristwatch and knead the dough until it hangs together with integrity.

Let it rise for 1 hour in a warm place. Cathy puts it in a bowl with a pillowcase laid over the top and lets it rise in her oven, which has a pilot light.

Punch it down.

Let it rise again for 45 minutes.

Knead it again.

Divide it into two loaves — either round ones on a cookie sheet or bread-shaped ones in breadpans.

Put the loaves on the top of the stove and let them rise again for half an hour while you preheat the oven.

Bake them in a 350° oven for 50-60 minutes, until they sound hollow when you tap them.

"This is very time intensive," Cathy tells me. "But it gives such a sense of accomplishment. Baking bread always seemed an insurmountable task but it's really very simple and creative. It's a wonderful way to provide for yourself and be able to share at the same time."

It warms my heart that Cathy has become a breadbaker, something I no longer make time for in my own kitchen. It also warms me that she is strong, forthright and my good friend, who keeps me politically aware and environmentally sound.

Thinking about bread and Cathy brings to mind how inextricably linked women are with food — both with its nurturing aspects and its disorders.

Food can be a symbol of radical change for women, too, as evidenced by Judy Grahn's spirited quote:

I swear it on my common woman's head
A common woman is as common
as a common loaf of bread
and will rise.

The fact that food has been such an intimate part of my life and my recovery keeps me firmly in touch with the safe, happy, spirited side of my inner child, her hand still secured in her grandmother's, her eyes still wandering longingly toward the pastries — and the answer.

Now I have the delightful job of collecting and editing recipes from colleagues in the helping professions. Maybe food evokes the inner child in everyone. Surely she (or he) pops up in many of the recipes in this book.

Food For Body And Soul is much more than just a cookbook. With each recipe for something to eat is a recipe for recovery, food for the soul — a wise saying, a touching story, a useful anecdote, an uplifting joke.

The major message that follows is that it's okay to feel safe and happy. It's okay to nurture yourself. It's okay to

want to be loved and appreciated while you're caring for others.

Above all, it's okay to have fun — to associate the rituals of eating with health and pleasure. Whether your tastes run to Flan or Chicken Anonymous, it's okay to practice the art of feeling good even while you are in the throes of your own recovery from pain.

Gina Ogden
Cambridge, Massachusetts

COMFORT FOODS

Emotional Sobriety Smoothie

— Karen Paine-Gernée and Terry Hunt, Ed.D. —

Karen Paine-Gernée and Terry Hunt, Ed.D., friends and work partners for the last 15 years, are authors of *Emotional Healing: A Program For Emotional Sobriety*. They teach workshops at Esalen Institute, Omega Institute, the New York Open Center, Interface Foundation and Hollyhock Farms. Terry is a psychologist and bioenergetic therapist in Boston, Massachusetts. Karen has a practice in Boulder, Colorado.

Terry and his wife, Gale, are parents to Evan (age 4) and Avery (age 2). Karen and her husband Rick have just about finished raising Alex (24), Megan (22) and Max (20). Making smoothies is a common family activity.

Terry and Karen are currently engaged in a new collaboration on a book to be called *Secrets To Tell, Secrets To Keep*.

We chose smoothies because they are nutritious, lo-cal and an easy way to get an energy boost when you need one. They are fun and delicious for kids of all ages.

Our only serious caveat: Don't use this or any food to make the pain go away. It doesn't work anyway, but only substitutes one form of suffering for another. Perhaps the child in you could not bear the feelings, but the adult is learning to stretch your emotional capacities.

The rainbow of feeling includes all the shades and shines brightly when there is no resistance. There are no "bad" feelings or "bad" smoothies.

This is *your* smoothie and it's OK if you want to eat it all yourself. But you might want to share what it felt like to make it, or even make one in collaboration with someone else.

Emotional Sobriety Smoothie

PRE-RECOVERY RECIPE:

Worry about making the smoothie.
Do it all at once.
Complicate it.
Expect perfection.
Doubt yourself.
Blame your parents for your self-doubt.
Involve everyone you know in making the smoothie.
Worry about past smoothies.

Agonize.
Punish yourself if you don't make it perfectly.

Try to find the meaning of your smoothie.
Don't ask for support.
Judge your smoothie.
Sexualize it.
Use your smoothie to dull your pain.

Emotional Sobriety Smoothie

POST-RECOVERY RECIPE:

Delight in creating your smoothie.
Have fun.
Improvise.
Trust your inner banana (voice) (self) (wisdom).
Let your inner child help.
Forget past smoothies.
Decide what you like.
Be creative.
Make the smoothie with feeling.
Open to the experience.
Claim your right to this smoothie.
Forgive it.
Ask a trusted friend what a *normal* smoothie is.
Take pleasure.
Let God make the smoothie.

SMOOTHIE INGREDIENTS

These are just suggestions, the actual ingredients are up to you. The key is to become clear about what you really want out of life — or in this case, your smoothie. Then ask yourself for it.

To a cup or so of soy milk, low-fat milk, yogurt, water or ice, add a cup or so of some of these fruits (or others):

Bananas
Strawberries
Apples
Pears
Nectarines
Peaches
Blueberries
Raspberries
Then add:
Nutritional yeast
Granola
Unsalted nuts of any kind.

Throw them in the blender nice and easy, one step at a time, and let the process happen.

Soothing Muffins
DAILY MEDITATION FOR FAST-TRACK LIVING

— Bryan E. Robinson, Ph.D. —

© *Mitchell Kearney*

Bryan E. Robinson, Ph.D., is an author, consultant and trainer in the recovery field and a professor at the University of North Carolina at Charlotte. He has written *Heal Your Self-Esteem: Recovery From Addictive Thinking; Soothing Moments: Daily Meditations For Fast-Track Living; Work Addiction: Hidden Legacies Of Adult Children; Stressed Out? A Guidebook For Taking Care Of Yourself* and *Healograms* plus eight other books on the family.

I make a batch of these muffins once a week. It is a favorite ritual I always look forward to. I usually choose a time in the week when I have been rush-houring and quick-stepping and need some time for contemplation.

Making these muffins is a soothing, meditative experience that helps me unwind and become calm and centered. As I mix the ingredients I consciously put positive, healing thoughts into the batter.

Eating the muffins is a healing experience, not only because they are full of natural ingredients, but also because, as I eat them, I receive the original healing that I put into the preparation.

For the past two years my breakfast has consisted of one "soothing" muffin every morning. When I travel, I take them with me everywhere I go — whether it's to the Amazon jungle, the beaches of Maui or Peoria. Everyone who has ever eaten one begs for the recipe, so here it is.

Soothing Muffins:
Daily Meditation For Fast-Track Living

From the Spic-and-Span Kitchen of
Bryan Robinson, Ph.D.

1½ cups Muesli
1 cup skim milk
½ cup whole wheat flour
½ cup white all-purpose flour
½ teaspoon baking soda
2 teaspoons baking powder
½ teaspoon salt
½ teaspoon ground cinnamon
1 egg
¼ cup vegetable oil
¼ cup honey
½ teaspoon vanilla
1 large handful chopped pecans
2 well-ripened bananas
½ medium sized apple
(or substitute any of the following for bananas and apple: apricots, nectarines, peaches, carrots, plums, whole blueberries, halved dark sweet cherries, straw-berries, raspberries.)

In a bowl combine Muesli and milk. Let stand 3 minutes or until liquid is absorbed.

In a separate bowl stir together flour, baking soda, baking powder, salt and cinnamon.

Into Muesli mixture, stir egg, oil, honey, vanilla and pecans.

Add bananas to Muesli mixture by squeezing them between your fingers. (Oh, what a feeling!) Then add apple cut in small chunks.

Add dry mixture and stir vigorously. Batter will be thick.

Use a 12-cup, well-greased muffin pan, filling to top of each cup. Bake in a 400° oven for 20 minutes.

Makes 12 muffins.

Make Soup, Not War

— Gina Ogden, Ph.D. —

Gina Ogden, Ph.D., is a recovering therapist. In addition to collecting and editing the recipes for *Food For Body And Soul*, she is the author of *Sexual Recovery: Everywoman's Guide Through Sexual Co-Dependency* and co-author of *Safe Encounters: How Women Can Say Yes To Pleasure And No To Unsafe Sex*.

Partly because of her involvement in this book and partly because she feels a meal that's to be shared in the eating is often best shared in the cooking, too, some of her friends have started calling her Lady Potluck. She has been called many things in her somewhat adventurous life, but this is a title she wears with pride.

I use soupmaking behavior to slow myself down when life begins whirling out of control. This is the soup I made the night U.S. planes started bombing Iraq. Aside from being therapeutic to prepare, it's delicious and healthy and people who eat it feel loved and nurtured and remember it for a long time.

Make Soup, Not War

Today, slow down and make some soup.
I don't mean out of a package,
I mean soup from scratch.
This means thinking about it first.
Intention.
Intentional soup.

How do you think about soup?
You can think about what to put in it:
    Onions.
    Carrots.
    Tomatoes.
    Love.

Don't forget the garlic —
to ward off bleak spirits.
A whole head of it maybe.
Peel the skins off
but leave the buds intact.

You can think about who's going to eat
this soup.
You. And maybe someone else.
This soup has to be special.

So simmer at least two big
chopped-up onions
in a good splash of olive oil
until the smells fill the house
and your stomach begins to smile.

Then cut up chunks of carrot
and a couple of fat tomatoes
(or out of season a biggish can of them)
the garlic buds . . ..

Throw these in the pot
with enough water to make it look like
Soup.

Put the lid on tight
and the fire way down low
and sit back and think again
about who's going to be eating it —
making soup can help you
imagine details that fill your heart.

Add the flavorings:
    Peppercorns.
    Curry.
    Vinegar.
    Tamari.

Simmer for a couple hours
more or less. Lift the lid
and take a deep sniff every half hour.
Deep enough to clear your sinuses.

Stir with love.

Heartwarming Lentil Stew

— Jonathan B. Weiss, Ph.D., and Laurie Weiss, M.A. —

Jonathan B. Weiss, Ph.D., and Laurie Weiss, M.A., have worked together as psychotherapists, marriage counselors and management consultants since 1971. Married in 1960, they have two grown children. Personally and professionally they have experienced, studied and taught about the growth and development of healthy interdependent relationships.

They are best known for their use of powerful regressive therapy techniques in an outpatient setting. Most of their clients are adult children of dysfunctional families.

They are the authors of *Recovery From Co-Dependency: It's Never Too Late To Reclaim Your Childhood.* Laurie is the author of *I Don't Need Therapy But . . .* and *An Action Plan For Your Inner Child: Parenting Each Other.*

After 30 years of marriage and 20 years of working together, we have found the following ingredients helpful in moving from a very co-dependent relationship to a mostly interdependent one:

- Know that loving each other *means* a commitment to your own and each other's growth.
- Recognize that unskillful behavior comes from ignorance, not evil, and often from unmet needs of the inner child.
- Ask for help when you need it, even from each other.
- Don't sweat the small stuff; it's all small stuff.
- Change is inevitable.

These are common sense items, the kinds of things children seem to do automatically if adults don't mess them up. For example:

Our two-year-old son Brian was enjoying the freedom to run around by himself in a large, open shopping mall when he met a clown for the first time. He was terrified; he ran back to us, screaming all the way. After a lot of comforting and explaining, he calmed down and we went on with the day.

Several months later we had just finished ordering our meals in a new restaurant when a clown walked into the room to entertain the customers. Our son took one look and dove under the table, hysterical, refusing to come out, even when we assured him that the clown was gone. He was so afraid the clown would come back that we had to leave.

Since his "irrational" fears were causing a problem for us, we decided to "cure" him. In the car we pooled our degrees and therapy skills and had a little session with him:

Mom & Dad: Brian, do you know what a clown really is?

Brian: Yes, a man with paint on his face.

M & D: Do you know why he paints his face?

B: To look funny.

M & D: Do you know that a clown won't hurt you?

B: Yes.

M & D: Brian, do you like being scared of clowns?

B: No!

M & D: Do you want us to help you not be scared?

B: Yes.

M & D: What can we do to help you not be scared of clowns?

B: You can put me in the car and take me to another restaurant where they don't have clowns!

For a heartwarming meal when *you're* scared of clowns (or even when you're not), here is a nurturing, hearty stew for a cold day. We like to eat it with fresh warm bread or bagels. We freeze the leftovers in serving-size portions to be thawed in the microwave when we don't have time to cook.

Heartwarming Lentil Stew

Chop into small pieces:
4 large onions
2-3 carrots

A food processor helps chop everything quickly, or chop with a sharp knife — and meditate — if you prefer.

Sauté these in a nonstick pan, without oil.

When onions are soft, add:
1 pound lentils
2 pounds chopped, canned tomatoes, with their liquid

6 cups stock or seasoned water
2 teaspoons thyme
2 teaspoons marjoram leaves
1½ teaspoons salt (or to taste)
2-3 teaspoons curry powder (optional)
½ cup chopped fresh parsley (optional)

Cover and simmer for 30-40 minutes, until the lentils are soft.

Serves 8-10.

My Bubby's Lukshen And Cheese

— Joy Miller, M.A., C.A.C. —

A connoisseur of high-fat foods and a good joke, Joy Miller, M.A., C.C.D., is founder and director of RENEWAL, the Center for Counseling and Personal Growth, in Peoria, Illinois. She has a private practice specializing in the treatment of children and adult children of alcoholics, co-dependency and relationship issues. She is also a consultant to the Illinois Heart Institute. A nationally known lecturer and trainer, she is the author of *My Holding You Up Is Holding Me Back*, *Addictive Relationships: Reclaiming Your Boundaries* and co-author of *Following The Yellow Brick Road: An Adult Child's Personal Journey Through Oz*. Her latest book, *Celebrations of Life*, will be out soon.

When I was a child, my Bubby (that's Grandma in Yiddish) showed her love by making me special dishes.

This is my Bubby's food of choice (drug of choice?). Quite simply, this Jewish tranquilizer is:

My Bubby's Lukshen And Cheese

Noodles (elbow, naturally)
Cook them and serve with:
    butter
    salt and pepper
    cottage cheese.

You can vary the proportions. You can add poppy seeds. You can add other kinds of cheese. You can add apple or pineapple, even. You can mix it up with beaten eggs and bake it in the oven with something crunchy on top.

But my Bubby nurtured my soul (through my stomach) the simple way. Eat it hot or cold. It will delight any small person — or a grown up with a willing and hungry inner child.

This is sure to produce results similar to Homemade Chicken Soup from Bubby. But that's another story.

It's rich and fattening, of course. Do you know anyone who was nurtured with a scrap of lettuce?

SALADS AND APPETIZERS

You Cannot Make This Salad Wrong

— Ruth Fishel, M.Ed., C.A.C. —

Ruth Fishel, M.Ed., C.A.C. has always followed a lifelong interest in helping people to express their feelings. She began with greeting cards and later shifted to *recovery* greeting cards as she became deeply committed to her own recovery.

As meditation became an important part of her recovery, she was drawn from a deep and irresistible place within to respond to people who resisted meditation. This is now her "calling" which has led her to write *The Journey Within: A Spiritual Path To Recovery, Learning To Live In The Now, Time For Joy* and *Healing Energy: The Power Of Recovery.*

The Gulf War has inspired her latest book, *5 Minutes For World Peace . . . Forever,* a 90-page meditation booklet soon to be expanded into a 365-page book, *Time For Peace.*

I love salad and have chosen to offer it for two main reasons.

First of all, as a typical textbook-case Libra, I often have a difficult time making choices around things that I like. Years ago I was the buyer for four recovery stores and I wanted to buy *everything* I liked because someone else might like it too and might want to buy it. I also wanted to put *everything*, and I do mean *everything*, up front in the stores so that *everyone* could see *everything* when they walked in the door. This, as you can well imagine, led to a very crowded and cluttered front part of the store and an empty and unattractive back. Broken and unpopular items usually ended up there on sale.

You can put *everything* into a salad too, but I've never seen one that looked cluttered. And you don't have to make hard and fast choices. You can vary it according to your whim, your taste, your pocketbook. You can enjoy it alone or with a crowd; you can have it any time of day or night. You can serve it at a fancy formal table or at a picnic at the beach.

The second reason I'm offering salad is that early in my own recovery from alcoholism, when my body and soul were screaming for another drink, any relief I could get was a welcome miracle. My jaw ached from clenching my teeth, my hands were always in fists and I could more often than not be found pacing.

A friend gave me some simple, profound advice. "Get a head of lettuce," she suggested. "Tear off one leaf at a time and concentrate as best you can on all aspects of that leaf. Wash it. Pat it dry. And then repeat the process until you've worked through the entire head of lettuce. Be aware of the texture of each leaf, listen to the sounds as you tear it from the main stem, to the sounds of running water and to the patting of the towel. Watch the droplets of water as they glisten on the leaf and then disappear."

Little did I know that this advice was a lesson in meditation and mindfulness, which I was to rediscover years later. Now I see it also as a lesson in patience and impulse control, as well as relief from tension and the basics for a wonderful salad.

The skills that we practice — mindfulness — can then be brought to other aspects of salad-making such as cutting and scraping. Practice mindfulness with the arranging of various colors and textures. Bring awareness to aromas and tastes. Mindfulness can begin as you select ingredients at the store or even earlier as you make a shopping list, if that's in your nature.

A therapeutic reverse of this process is helpful if you're feeling angry or resentful or frustrated. *Rip* the lettuce apart. Yell and scream as you tear it in pieces, a leaf at a time or by the fistful. Toss the salad with your hands, shake it and imagine anyone you wish as you *express your feelings.*

You Cannot Make This Salad Wrong

Possible salad ingredients are endless:
Lettuce: red leaf, green leaf, iceberg, also spinach, chicory and sprouts
Tomatoes and cucumbers
Celery, radishes and mushrooms, thinly sliced
Peppers, green, yellow and red
Olives, black and green
Artichoke hearts
Shredded cheese and hard-boiled eggs
Tuna or coldcuts
Croutons
Fruit, sliced or cubed
All kinds of seasoning, herbs, spices and lots of garlic.

Edible flowers like nasturtiums and squash blossoms are an exotic, romantic addition and a great conversation piece.

Mix with your favorite dressing and enjoy each delicious bite, mindfully, remembering that *you cannot make this salad wrong.*

Affirming The Senses

Allowing yourself to be mindful during the preparation of salads or any other food can be a transformational experience. Here is an affirmation to help heighten awareness:

All my senses are awake and alive in this moment and, as I bring my full attention to the textures and smells and sounds and tastes and colors and shapes around me, I can feel my entire body begin to relax.

I nurture myself by connecting fully with the process of blending and measuring, tasting and smelling.

Nothing is more important than exactly what I'm doing at this moment.

As I focus on the moment, tension and stress pour out of me with ease.

Peace and tranquility flow through me.

Every breath I take reminds me of how complete I am. I can smile, knowing that I deserve this time for me to become centered and peaceful and to enjoy.

This moment is mine to enjoy fully.

My body and soul are at peace.

Intentional Salad Dressing

— Susan Cooley Ricketson, Ph.D. —

Susan Cooley Ricketson, Ph.D., author of *The Dilemma Of Love*, has been featured on national television, on radio shows and in newspaper articles. She is a psychotherapist in Connecticut where she conducts workshops, lectures and writes articles on co-dependency.

This is a salad dressing I invented when I needed to clean out my diet and help myself get well from a variety of ailments. It is very good for cleansing every known toxin, including *candida*.

I make it when I travel. And wherever I have introduced it, people want the recipe. It has been a delight to share it with so many during the past years. May you enjoy all of the blessings it offers and live your journey to the fullest with an open compassionate heart.

Intentional Salad Dressing

Mix together:

¹/₃ cup freshly squeezed, strained lemon juice

²/₃ cup pure, cold-pressed olive oil

½ teaspoon granulated garlic

½ teaspoon onion powder

½ teaspoon dill weed

Dash of Spice Island salad seasoning for oil and vinegar dressing

Vary proportions to taste . . . and enjoy!

Note: This dressing must be used right away. If you want to store it, substitute vinegar for the lemon juice — but know that even though it tastes delicious, it no longer has the same kind of cleansing properties.

This dressing is delicious on almost anything you can think of. I use it on pasta and tofu. Tofu, by the way, is high in calcium. I was told by a holistic doctor that if you can develop a daily taste for tofu, you don't have to worry about calcium loss at menopause. It's also high in *chi* energy — the earth energy that's lacking in so many people who are high achievers and live upstairs in their heads.

Mostly, though, I use this dressing on salad.

Here are the ingredients for a cleansing salad. Note the absence of *candida*-forming vegetables like mushrooms and tomatoes. All of the ingredients here promote health and light. Wash them well to remove any chemicals or molds.

Start with green or red leaf lettuce.

Cut up to suit: broccoli, cauliflower, carrots, celery, radishes, zucchini, yellow squash, scallions.

Garnish with fresh herbs: parsley, cilantro, arugula.

If you make this salad and dressing with love, self-caring and a sense of discovery, its ingredients will promote moderation, flexibility, cleansing and quality of life, which encourage groundedness to our Earth Mother. Trust in your inner guidance as you create it with intention and consciousness.

The garnishes can remind you of God's special gifts, given freely each day if we but notice them and take them in. The dressing can bring you spontaneity and enthusiasm — breathe fully into them.

The entire repast has balance. Preparing and eating it can help you focus on actively taking in what is healthy, instead of merely avoiding negatives. See, smell and taste as you listen with love, joyously sharing intimately with yourself and/or others.

Cosmic Treats

— Patricia O'Gorman, Ph.D. —

Patricia O'Gorman, Ph.D., is a psychologist, lecturer and author. She is director of the Adult Child Counseling Center in East Greenbush, New York.

She directed the Division of Prevention for the National Institute on Alcohol Abuse and Alcoholics and was co-founder of the National Association for Children of Alcoholics (NACoA), and founding director of the National Council on Alcoholism, Department of Prevention and Education.

She has co-authored *Breaking The Cycle Of Addiction*, a parenting handbook for Adult Children of Alcoholics, and *12 Steps To Self-Parenting* (book and audiotape). *Self-Parenting 12-Step Workbook* is her newest book.

I believe that we are all connected to each other and responsible for each other and also for Mother Earth.

It's not hard to develop a cosmic imagination . . .

First, imagine being in your home.

Now, imagine flying over your home.

Next, imagine yourself over the town or city where you live and, as you now fly higher, imagine you can see the whole region where you live. As you fly higher still, you can see the outline of your country.

Finally, as you leave the Earth's atmosphere, you can see Mother Earth spinning in space, just one of the Creator's many planets in a wondrous cosmos full of planets and suns. Let yourself feel the delicacy of Mother Earth. Open your heart to her and commit yourself to feeling your love for her.

Feel your gratitude to the Creator for all the gifts you have been given. And as you descend back to Mother Earth, allow yourself to feel your kinship with all living things and the elements.

• Commit yourself to doing one thing each day to help someone else, and not telling anyone about it.

• Commit yourself to showing your love to one child still lost in the chaos of addiction and abuse.

• Commit yourself and know that God's Will will be done through you.

There are so many ways we can reach out to one another and nurture each other. One of these ways is through food. When my husband, Robert, and I were getting to know each other, he gave a dinner party for me and did the cooking. A man who could cook! What a gift! That evening got me beyond my belief system that said I have to do it all.

Here is the Wow recipe that helped make our connection.

Cosmic Treats

All you need is: Bacon strips, Pitted dates, Toothpicks
Wrap 1 bacon strip around each pitted date and secure with a toothpick. Put under the broiler until they are crisp. Sweet and salty — *yum!*

Mother's Canapes For Courage

— Ellen Ratner, Ed.M. —

Ellen Ratner, Ed.M., has been working in the mental health and substance abuse fields for the last 17 years. She is author of *The Other Side Of The Family* and director of the ARC Research Foundation in Rockville, Maryland, where she is conducting research on substance abuse and factors such as child abuse that affect treatment outcomes.

My mother loved to cook. When she moved to New York at the age of 50, she took every cooking lesson given by master chefs. Her caring and love for others were expressed in her sharing of this passion.

Always practical, she could make a gourmet meal and yet use short-cuts when she thought them necessary. My favorite was her "fancy French fry" recipe. She would go out, get McDonald's French fries, dip them in hot oil for 30 seconds and, presto! the best French fries you've ever tasted.

Gracious and fun entertaining was her specialty. Frequently — to save work, such as polishing silver and housecleaning — she would give dinner parties on two successive nights. She loved color, and the food she made was a favor to the eye as well as to the palate.

At the age of 54 she was diagnosed with cancer. As part of her life-affirmation, she decided to embark on an effort to see if, in her words, she could "beat the clock" by beginning a series of plans for entertaining and dinner parties. When she announced this to her therapist, she was told that she was in denial of her illness. Undaunted, she wrote eight of these plans and published and promoted the first one while on chemotherapy, before she became too ill to continue.

During her illness she was able to use her cooking to get closer to our family. She taught my brother the mysteries of Chinese cooking, and always found the strength to have our favorite foods available when we would visit. Her cooking served as her bridge between life and death and continues to serve our family as her legacy.

Here are two of her unpublished recipes:

CHOPPED LIVER

This old favorite may be used as a canape or first course. The garnishes suggested may be changed according to your own likes and dislikes: tomato wedges, cucumber slices, carrot curls, celery sticks and olives are but a few that may be used. Make it colorful and attractive.

1 pound chicken livers
1 medium onion, thinly sliced
3 tablespoons chicken fat, butter or margarine (I prefer chicken fat)
2 hard-boiled eggs
Salt
Pepper
Sweet onion
Garlic-dill pickles
Italian bread, crackers or party rye bread

Broil (on foil) the chicken livers, turning until they are lightly browned.

In a small skillet, sauté the onions in chicken fat; set aside.

Using a meat grinder or a chopping bowl and chopping knife, grind or chop very fine the hard-boiled eggs, sautéed onions and chicken livers.

Taste for salt and pepper. Livers should be very well seasoned.

You may have to add a little more chicken fat or melted butter to make the mixture moist.

As a canape, serve it in a bowl surrounded with rye bread, crackers, sweet onion rings and pickles.

As a first course, arrange the chopped liver on a lettuce leaf on individual plates and garnish with sweet onion rings and pickles. Serve with heated Italian bread.

CREAM CHEESE AND CAVIAR TRAY

This looks and tastes expensive, but is both economical and a quickie to make.

1 8-ounce package cream cheese, softened to room temperature
1 small jar black lumpfish caviar (this is not the expensive kind)
1 cup egg salad
1 red or Bermuda onion, chopped fine
1 medium jar pimiento stuffed olives, drained
Assorted crackers

In the middle of a large platter, place the bar of cream cheese.

Spread a half-inch layer of the lumpfish caviar on top.

Surround the cheese and caviar with mounds of egg salad, chopped onion, olives and crackers.

Hummus For Persistence

— Charles L. Whitfield, M.D. —

Charles L. Whitfield, M.D., is the author of *Healing The Child Within, A Gift To Myself: A Personal Workbook And Guide To Healing My Child Within, Co-Dependence — Healing The Human Condition: The New Paradigm For Helping Professionals And People In Recovery* and *Boundaries And Relationships In Recovery.*

He has been a pioneer in the field of addiction, medicine and recovery since the early 1970s. He works with a skilled and caring group of therapists at Whitfield associates in Baltimore. There he co-leads therapy groups for adult children, and chemical dependents and sees people in individual psychotherapy weekly. He delivers talks and workshops nationally on key areas of recovery.

In my work as a psychotherapist and in my own recovery I am continually impressed by the courage and persistence that it takes to do the work of recovery. *But it does work.* We can get free of our unnecessary pain and suffering and create a more fulfilling life for ourselves.

Recipe For Recovery

1. Getting to know and live from and as my True Self or Child Within, as opposed to letting my false self run my life. This task includes (a) learning to live from my *inner life*, which includes (b) learning about my *feelings* and how to use them.

2. Learning about *age regression* (when I suddenly feel little and helpless) and how to heal it.

3. Learning to *grieve* my ungrieved hurts, losses and traumas.

4. Learning to *tolerate* and *handle* emotional pain.

5. Learning to set healthy *boundaries.*

6. Learning to get my *needs* met.

7. Working through my *core* recovery issues.

The final two tasks come later in recovery, where we become progressively more spiritually aware:

8. Learning that the core of my being is *love.*

9. In concert with my Higher Power, becoming a *co-creator* of my life.

Throughout this process, and especially in the latter stages, we can experience and learn a profound wisdom, part of which is reflected in the following statement from *A Course In Miracles,* which is a modern holy book that many people in recovery are beginning to study.

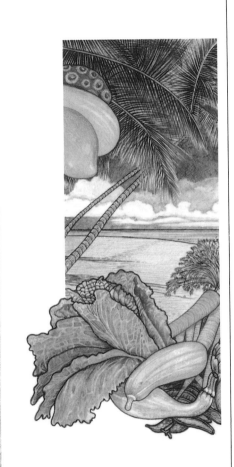

I am responsible for what I see.
I choose the feelings I experience, and I decide upon the goal I would achieve.
And everything that seems to happen to me I ask for and receive as I have asked.

The only one who can take this responsibility and make our life work is our True Self, our Child Within.

Our false self is incapable of running our life successfully. We make our life work first by healing our self so that we *know* our self and can live from and *as* our True Self. Then we can choose the God of our understanding to assist us in co-creating our life.

The only way to fill our emptiness is thus by realizing our True Self and then experientially connecting it to God. We cannot fill our emptiness with anything outside of ourself, not any person, place, thing, behavior or experience. Not even with food. But we can get physical nourishment from healthy foods.

One of my favorites is Middle Eastern food, and one of the healthiest of these is hummus. This can be used as a spread, dip or to mix into nearly any kind of food.

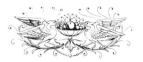

Hummus For Persistence

1 can chickpeas (garbanzo beans)
1 tablespoon olive oil
1 tablespoon cumin
1-2 tablespoons garlic powder
Juice of 2 fresh lemons or limes
(bottled juice is okay, but is not an
ideal substitute)
5 tablespoons sesame tahini
Garnish: 2 tablespoons olive oil
1-2 teaspoons cumin
a small handful chopped fresh
parsley
Pour chickpeas and half their water
into a blender.
Add olive oil, cumin, garlic powder,

lemon or lime juice and tahini.

Blend to a thick, creamy paste. If it is too thick, or if all the beans are not fully ground, add a little more water and blend again.

Pour into a bowl. On the top add another 2 tablespoons of olive oil, sprinkle 1 or 2 teaspoons of cumin and chopped fresh parsley.

Just writing out this recipe, which I learned from my Middle Eastern friend Alice Kiljian, makes my mouth water for a dish of hummus. Excuse me while I go and prepare one. And enjoy yours if you decide to try it.

LIGHTNESS OF BEING

Homecoming Curry

— Marie Stilkind —

Marie Stilkind has been an editor of books and magazines for the past 30 years, and has been senior editor at Health Communications for the last five. Fortunately she is a compulsive reader and a scavenger of unrelated facts. She is a seeker who was intensely interested in the recovery movement even before she knew it had a name. Working for Health Communications has been a gift she never expected but is very grateful for.

To get to the holy island of Iona in Scotland you need to take a three-day pilgrimage. First, you take a 9-hour international flight to London. From there you take a domestic flight to Glasgow. When you get to Glasgow airport, you have to get to Queen Street Railway Station to sit in the station for two hours, admire the Victorian architecture, eat stale cheese sandwiches and drink very strong tea.

Finally the train to the western highlands and Oban arrives. The train is computerized so naturally half-way there it breaks down — at Crianlarich, a tiny little town with an equally small railway station, which naturally does not serve food or drink and which naturally is having the lavatories remodeled so that they are not available to the passengers who have to sit there for four hours. We are, however, surrounded by the western highlands and the scenery is breathtakingly beautiful. It is now past eleven (we were due in Oban at eight) and the sun is starting to go down. It goes down late in Scotland in June. And it is getting very cold. We cannot sit in the broken-down train because they are afraid it might blow up so we huddle in the tiny waiting room.

Finally an old steam train which had been put out to pasture comes chuff-chugging into Crianlarich.

When we get into Oban, it is after midnight. Pitch dark and no buses or taxis out this late. No one is around. I walk to the hotel dragging my suitcases and praying that the hotel is still open. Fortunately it is and there is even heat in the bedroom. I've been on the go now for 48 hours so as soon as I put my head down, I am asleep.

The next morning's breakfast is served in an old-fashioned dining room, straight out of a 1930s Agatha Christie movie with waitresses in white caps and aprons. Being famished and not having eaten a meal since the plastic food on the flight from the States, I am hoping for kippers or kidneys, but instead am served cold cereal, tea and toast.

With stomach still grumbling, I go off to find the ferry to Craignure on the Isle of Mull. I manage to drag my suitcases up the gangplank and we sail off to Mull on a clear blue sea. This time all I can find is another strong cup of tea and some Scottish shortbread. I'm so desperate I get two packets.

At Craignure I come rushing down

the gangplank with the suitcases hurtling down the steep incline. I am first in line to the bus that will take me to the other end of the island of Mull to Fionphort. Bumping through the most beautiful scenery in the world: rolling hills, green vales, woolly sheep and frolicking lambs all delight the eye and even make me forget the growls and grumbles of my near-empty stomach. At Fionphort we have to wait for the ferry to take us to Iona. This ferry is very small and primitive but fortunately the trip is not long.

Finally ashore, after wading through sea water with my suitcases rolling behind me, I make for Duncraig, the ecumenical retreat house where I will stay. The herring gulls scream over my head, welcoming me to Iona. The sheep stare at me with their startled, surprised looks. They wander all over the road. No cars are allowed on Iona and the roads belong to the sheep.

At last I reach Duncraig. Am I too late for lunch? Will Sue Daniels have anything for me to eat or will I have to make do with another cup of tea until dinner? I open the front door and can smell the most heavenly scent of curry.

"Sue, I'm here!" I shout.

"Please, God, let the curry be for me!" I pray. It is. And simmering on the stove in that sunlit kitchen is the best meal I have ever eaten. And here is the recipe for you.

Homecoming Curry

CALEDONIAN CURRY
(Iona Style)

1 lb. lean ground round (or turkey hamburger)

1 large onion, chopped into small pieces

1 small apple, cut into small squares

1 clove garlic, minced

3 tablespoons raisins

2 tablespoons curry powder

¼ teaspoon ginger powder

1 small container plain yogurt

½ cucumber, chopped

1 can sweet peas (drained)

Cook ground round (you can substitute turkey hamburger if you wish) with chopped onion until meat is brown.

Pour off excess fat.

Cook apple, garlic, raisins with curry and ginger in yogurt. Simmer for 10 minutes.

Add sweet peas and cucumber, mix, and pour over meat. Stir together with wooden spoon. Simmer for five minutes.

Serve with rice and canned stewed tomatoes. In Scotland they also serve this with potatoes instead of rice.

Food For The Soul

Why do I travel all that way from Miami to the tiny island of Iona in the Hebrides? Why travel for three days? After the huff and puff of daily life, it's not that I want to go, it's that I *have* to.

Iona is a holy island which was a spiritual place even before St. Columba and his monks landed there in 563 A.D., before the Scottish kings (including Duncan and MacBeth) were buried there. Iona is known as a "very thin place, where there's very little between you and God."

The old abbey that was built in the eleventh century on the site of St. Columba's church has now been rebuilt and is run by the Iona Community, an ecumenical group that seeks to help people in need. Pilgrims from all over the world come to feel the peace of the island, attend services at the abbey and just generally sightsee and wander.

On Iona, God is. Each person hears her or his own need addressed and when they have to leave, they are restored and rededicated. It only takes an hour and the stress of years drops away. Even more than being fed by the Caledonian curry, I was nourished with the gift of at-oneness. I arrived a strung-out wreck, I left whole and complete. As Anthony de Mello says, "Nothing had changed but my attitude. Everything had changed."

(If you want to go to Iona, too, write Iona Cornerstone Foundation, Box HH, Falmouth, MA 02541 or The Head Resident, Duncraig, Isle of Iona, Argyll PA76 6SP, Scotland.)

Turn-It-Over Fish Stew

— Jo Chaffee, M.A. —

Jo Chaffee, M.A., is a therapist who practices in a community substance abuse agency in Quincy, Massachusetts. She was co-founder and editor of *Berkshire Women's News*. Her career in food has included cooking for a living, editing *The Berkshire Community Cookbook* and dispensing tea and sympathy for 20 years to boarding school students. She thinks of cooking as a relaxing recreational activity now that her sense of self-worth is no longer hooked to the outcome.

Long ago and far away, back before my daughter was born 26 years ago, I came across a recipe in the *New York Times* for fish stew. This must have been in Craig Claiborne's pre-cholesterol-concern days because it contains butter and milk and salt, and is absolutely delicious.

But what interests me about it in the context of recovery is not so much its lineage or its ingredients, but how my approach toward making it has changed over the years.

I compulsively followed the recipe, which called for 18 different ingredients and 47 separate steps and activities, including chopping, mincing, grinding, grating, melting, simmering, stirring, watching and flaking.

In those early days I thoroughly enjoyed gathering all those ingredients and getting out my mincers, snippers, choppers, grinders and graters. All that chop-chop, toss-toss and compulsive attention to minutiae allowed me to believe that I was being a good cook, which in my family was a badge of worthiness and a ticket of membership into the clan.

But times have changed and, fortunately, so have I. Although I have kept most of the gadgets (in a carefully labeled box in the attic) and still have the original *Times* recipe (and a photocopy on longer-lasting paper), I have shed much of the compulsiveness.

Nowadays my family and I often share a delicious modernization of this notion of fish stew — a version that bespeaks my focus on simplifying my life while retaining basic pleasures. I no longer need to feel so rigidly in control of everything; I am learning to turn it over.

This recipe is so simple that you may be skeptical of its deliciousness. Take a chance!

Turn-It-Over Fish Stew

1 or 2 big white onions, coarsely chopped
A dollop of olive oil or safflower oil
Half a lemon (optional)
1 or 2 big tomatoes, coarsely chopped (or a can of plum tomatoes, drained)
2 to 4 thick cod fillets (preferably fresh, but frozen works fine)

Salt and pepper and possibly curry powder to taste.

In a large frying pan, sauté the onions in the oil a few minutes, stirring to separate the chunks.

I sometimes squeeze half a lemon into this and throw the whole reamed-out rind in (you might want to remove it before serving). My partner sometimes adds the lightest touch of curry powder when sautéeing the onions.

Add the tomatoes, the cod, the salt and pepper.

Cover, and let it all gently stew on top of the stove for 10 or at the most 15 minutes, until the tomatoes are squishy and the cod flakes easily but still holds firmly together.

Served like this, we call this entree "Portuguese Cod" — since it resembles what we had in a Portuguese restaurant once on vacation. But if you add some water and stew it a little longer until the tomatoes get squishier and the cod flakier, you end up with more of a soup: "Cod Stew."

Both are good with some cut-up potatoes added in with the onions, and they both look better with some chopped parsley on top.

You can eat this right away, or make it ahead and reheat as you wish. You can freeze it and bring a big lump of it to a potluck weekend in the country, where it will serve 10. Reheated, the flavors all go together better; fresh is, well, fresh.

Ser-en-dip-i-ty:
The faculty of making happy and unexpected discoveries by accident.

— American Heritage
Dictionary

10 Simple Things You Can Do
To Feed Your Soul

• Listen to someone tell you a story and allow yourself to be moved by what is said . . . or left unsaid.

• Listen to your own heart today. Is it singing or sobbing? Maybe it's resting. Just listen and accept.

• Look at a leaf. Keep looking until you understand exactly how it feels to be a leaf.

• Give away something of value — to someone of value. It could be money. It could be words or ideas. It could be a home-cooked meal. It could be time. Feel what value feels like as it dances back and forth between friends.

• Play with a child — yours or someone else's. Remember what it's like to laugh.

• Organize your closet. Come out of your closet for a minute if you happen to be in it.

• Make some music. You don't have to be a musician to create a joyful noise — bang on pots and pans if you must. Let your music touch your soul.

• List all the people you love.

• Wear a vibrant color.

• Breathe for the pleasure of breathing.

Healing Veggies And Yang Nuts

— Jane Wright, R.P.T. —

Jane Wright, R.P.T., is a licensed physical therapist in Sheffield, Massachusetts. She uses intuition, as well as clinical skills, to access and balance the reasons that combine to create physical dysfunction in adult children from alcoholic and addictive homes and others.

When a person abuses alcohol, the liver is affected. Liver damage is not confined only to the alcoholic, however; it can be passed down to the children and the children's children. In my practice I've learned that it takes four generations of sobriety for the liver to thoroughly recover. That means that anyone who comes from an alcoholic family family may have a liver that is low-functioning and vulnerable to disease.

Anger is the emotion most clearly connected to the liver. When the liver is under-energized, people find themselves expressing anger in some pretty inappropriate ways.

You can help detox and heal your liver (and your anger) by frequent baths, particularly at the end of the day. You can also help by eating in a balanced way that doesn't add strain to the liver — the strain of a fat-rich diet is considerable. Try the following:

• You can warm your liver in preparation for food by drinking warm broth before eating. A few sips are sufficient.

• You can eat your daily protein before three in the afternoon. Protein is difficult to digest and will account for difficulty in remembering your dreams, as well as affecting the content, making

them less coherent and meaningful. Eating protein early in the day will calm your dreams and bring their meaning to the light of consciousness.

• You can eat your daily sweets after three in the afternoon. This is the easiest time for the liver to handle them.

• You can follow a low-fat diet. I like the following recipes because they're easy to make and quite festive, as well as easy on the recovering liver.

Healing Veggies And Yang Nuts

SQUASH BALLS

Steam a yellow winter squash (acorn, butternut, etc).

Scoop it out of its skin and mix it with chopped onions and enough flour so that you can form it into balls.

Add whatever seasoning you like: parsley, thyme, marjoram, ginger root — let yourself be imaginative.

Roll the squash balls in the Yang Nuts, below, and bake in a 350° oven for 15-20 minutes.

RICE BALLS

Mold cooked brown rice into balls while it is still warm and moist but not so hot it burns your hand.

Put a surprise in the middle of each ball: a umeboshi plum, a chunk of steamed carrot or broccoli.

Roll the rice balls in the Yang Nuts below and bake in a 350° oven for 15-20 minutes.

YANG NUTS

Nuts and seeds are delicious and a great source of protein, but they're usually too yin (expansive), which is hard on the liver. However, you can yangize (contract and balance) them like this:

Start with about a cupful of almonds, pecans or hazelnuts.

Put them through a seed grinder or chop them very fine with a sharp knife.

Cook them in a dry pan on top of the stove for a few minutes, stirring them until they turn slightly brown. Watch them carefully so they don't burn.

Add a few shakes of umeboshi vinegar (a macrobiotic vinegar you can buy in a shaker bottle in your healthfood store). This adds a salty but tangy taste. Don't add so much that the nuts get soggy (if they do, don't worry — they dry quickly after stirring a few minutes more).

You can also use pumpkin seeds in the same way, but don't grind them. Put them right in the pan and pour on the vinegar when they start to pop.

Use these Yang Nuts to roll your veggie balls in or sprinkle them on any food for a treat full of health and crunch.

A Blade Of Grass Pushing Against An Obstacle

— From the *I Ching*
The Ancient Chinese *Book Of Changes*

Times of growth are beset with difficulties. They resemble a first birth. But these difficulties arise from the very profusion of all that is struggling to attain form. Everything is in motion. Therefore if one perseveres that is a prospect of great success, in spite of the existing danger. When it is one's fate to undertake such new beginnings, everything is still unformed, dark. Hence one must hold back, because any premature move might mean disaster. Likewise, it is very important not to remain alone; in order to overcome the chaos one needs helpers. This is not to say, however, that one should look on passively at what is happening. One must lend one's hand and participate with inspiration and guidance.

Wild West Empowerment Chili

— Diane M. Laut and Jane Middelton-Moz, M.S., C.C.D. —

Diane M. Laut (left) owns DML Associates, and is the business manager for Jane Middelton-Moz and Griefwork Associates.

Jane Middelton-Moz is a teacher, lecturer and psychotherapist with over 20 years experience in the treatment of mental health and substance abuse problems. Currently living in Montpelier, Vermont, she is well known nationally and internationally for her work with adult children of alcoholics, children of trauma, multigenerational sexual and physical abuse, multi-generational grief, ethnic and cultural awareness and cultural self-hate.

She is co-author of *After The Tears: Reclaiming The Personal Losses Of Childhood* and author of *Children Of Trauma: Rediscovering Your Discarded Self* and *Shame And Guilt: The Masters Of Disguise.*

Wild West Empowerment Chili

INGREDIENTS FOR CHILI	INGREDIENTS FOR A BALANCED LIFE
1 pound dry kidney beans	Health
1½ quarts cold water	Time alone
4 tablespoons butter or margarine	Being with children
1 tablespoon flour	Community interest
1 large onion, sliced	
¼ cup green pepper, diced	Play
1 clove garlic, minced	
1 teaspoon chili powder	
1 teaspoon salt	Spirituality
2 1-pound cans of tomatoes	Friends
¼ cup cheese, shredded	School and work
½ teaspoon pepper, white or black	Family of origin
1 pound chuck steak, cubed (optional)	Significant other (optional)

Beans are the foundation of your chili.

The foundation of a balanced life is emotional and physical health.

Cook them until they're tender in the water — then drain them and set them aside until the sauce is done.

In life, it is good to step aside to take some time alone. It helps provide personal balance for the day.

Butter or margarine adds richness to your chili. Melt it in a large pot.

Add richness to your life by spending time with children — your own or others'.

Stir in flour, which will bind the ingredients together.

Bond to your world by being actively interested in your community.

For wonderful taste and spice, add onions, green pepper, garlic and chili powder. Cook until tender.

Spice up your spirit with play.

Add salt — a commodity worth more than gold in many cultures.

Stir in tomatoes for joyful color and flavor.

Spirituality means knowing the true meaning of things, and hence their true worth.

Add cheese for stick-to-your-ribs solidity.

Friendships provide color, flavor and joy.

Add black pepper — enough for a friendly taste, but not so much it catches in your throat. Let your individual taste determine the correct amount.

Life's solidity and stability come from school and work.

Time spent with family of origin can be both a pleasure and a pain. Setting personal limits on demands allows us to appreciate fully what can be offered.

— OPTIONAL —

Stir in browned cubed steak.

A significant other may be an option for your life . . . but make sure you know you can stand alone first.

Mix all ingredients gently together
for a Wild West chili . . . and a balanced life.

Empathic Pasta Sauce

— Teri Miller —

Teri Miller has been the executive assistant of Health Communications, Inc., for ten years. An adult child of totally dysfunctional everything, she has become, in recovery, a discerning spectator of life. She describes herself as a couch potato who likes to go for an occasional swim.

As a kid it was my mother and me. After working two jobs, or practicing her alcoholism, there wasn't much home cooking. Most often I'd come home to an empty house and find five bucks on the table for dinner.

Growing up in Philadelphia, land of the best soft pretzels, hoagies, steak sandwiches and Tastykakes, five bucks could go a long way. My favorite "dinner" was Pepsi and Wise potato chips (the dark ones), a hoagie or steak sandwich and a black/white milkshake, with mint chocolate chip ice cream for dessert.

Today as an adult I don't often relate food to nurturing. I can just as easily go without eating and would love it if science just came up with a pill to take daily.

But my mother did have a few nurturing moments and so do I. If there's someone to cook for, my German/Irish mother's Italian sauce is always a hit. It takes a while to make but when I'm in the mood, it's a great way to spend the day. It feels like taking care of myself and my little kid inside.

This sauce is great on pasta, or you can eat it all by itself in soup bowls, with bread and a green salad. Not bad for someone who doesn't relate to food, eh?

As always, as I explore more about myself, I understand my mother a bit better, too. I can empathize with her not wanting to make home-cooked food every day. If I had to concoct this pasta sauce regularly, I'd vote for leaving five bucks on the table every once in a while, too.

Empathic Pasta Sauce

2 large cans peeled tomatoes
4 small cans tomato paste
1 small can tomato sauce
½ teaspoon sugar or 3 tablespoons honey
Salt (to taste)
Pepper (to taste)
Fresh oregano (to taste)
¼ cup olive oil
2 onions, cut in chunks
2 fresh garlic cloves
1 green pepper
1-2 pounds tofu
or 1 Italian sausage (hot)
1 pound ground beef
1 onion, finely diced
1 egg
¼ cup bread crumbs

This sauce simmers for no less than four hours. And so you'll need a tall pot. The higher the sauce can rise, the richer it will taste. I avoid using an aluminum pot because the acid in the tomatoes will cause the aluminum to leach — and aluminum in your system can cause health problems.

Crush the peeled tomatoes, add the tomato paste, tomato sauce, sugar or honey, salt, pepper, oregano and olive oil.

Bring to a boil, stirring often.

Cover and turn to low.

In a fry pan with some more olive oil, fry onions, garlic and green peppers.

Add to sauce and stir well.

Add a bit of water to the sauce as it's simmering if it gets too thick.

My mother's recipe calls for sausage and meatballs. When I was a vegetarian, I left these out and put in a pound or two of diced-up tofu instead to add some body. Tofu should be added during the last 15 minutes of the cooking.

If you are using sausage, pierce it with a fork. In a fry pan, cover the sausage with water and cover the pan with a lid. Cook over medium heat until the water is gone. Turn sausage and add more water; cover and cook until the water evaporates.

Cut the sausage into bite-size pieces and add it to the sauce.

Put the ground beef in a bowl. Add the egg and bread crumbs and some finely diced onion, oregano, salt and pepper. Mix well and form meatballs.

Fry the meatballs in olive oil until they are crispy on the outside.

Add the meatballs to the sauce along with some of the juice. If you cook them in the sauce for more than about a half an hour, they fall apart. Then you have meat sauce instead of tomato sauce with meatballs.

Continue to simmer the sauce, adding water and more seasonings as needed. It can simmer all day long, but not less than four hours. If you want to freeze it, let it sit refrigerated overnight before freezing.

Chicken Anonymous

— Yvonne Kaye, Ph.D. —

Yvonne Kaye, Ph.D., a columnist and radio talk show host, is author of *The Child That Never Was* and *Credit, Cash And Co-Dependency.*

Motto: Life is grim but not necessarily serious. Owes personal recovery to laughing a lot, listening to people whose opinions really matter, and currently living in a happy state of arrogance.

Goal: To be eccentric and outrageous. Yeah! Having dealt with my own mourning, I recognize that laughter is the great healer.

If there were recipes for humor, I would write them something like:

Take two loud giggles every morning. Dissolve in a cup of fun.

Add one spoken "I love you, Yvonne." Mix with a strong self-hug.

Make sure the cup is big, with a quotation such as: "An ounce of irreverence is worth a pound of serious thought."

Mix thoroughly in a closed container whilst dancing.

Drink slowly and if you can develop short term hiccups that should create more laughter and if someone catches you doing all this, so much the better.

Set aside at least ½ hour per day to be silly.

Imagine yourself in a pure light of protection with arrows of negativity coming at you and bouncing off into the Universe.

That's the recipe for *Normal*.

Chicken Anonymous

How do you make a chicken feed ten people? In my early poverty days, this was a good one.

One broiled chicken, boned.

Tear into pieces (I don't mean verbally; sarcasm hurts).

Cook white or brown rice, enough for ten.

Cut up two green peppers in frying pan. Add cooked rice and torn chicken. Fry for a few minutes and no one will know what they are eating, but it looks as if you have been in the kitchen for hours. Tell them you have. The anonymous chicken tastes better with guilt.

A variation on Chicken Anonymous is:

SEX EDUCATION WITH CURRY

When my eldest daughter was six, she decided she wanted to know the facts of life. Being a very responsible but strange parent, I decided to go to any lengths so that she would be knowledgeable and all her questions would be answered. I drew pictures, told stories, invited questions. I felt wonderful that I could have such an open and loving relationship with my child and knew that I had done a fantastic job. At that moment I was preparing a curry dish for the seven European students who were living with us. Being a woman, of course I could do both things at the same time and was delighted with my accomplishments.

When everyone trooped in for dinner that night, I served a magnificent curry with great pride. The slight problem was that I forgot the fruit, the curry powder and the rice. Apart from that, what tasted like a mashed meatloaf certainly was different.

It turned out my daughter simply wanted to know where she had come from, not how she got there. She shared at this extraordinary meal that, "Mum was really weird today, drawing funny pictures when I only wanted to know if I came from London." Just like the co-dependent I was, giving, giving, giving, no boundaries. She confessed later that she knew it all anyway. Nice kid.

You can follow up these chicken dishes with:

RASPBERRY SURPRISE

1 sponge cake (either made or bought)
1 pint fresh raspberries *or* 1 large package frozen raspberries, *or* 1 large can raspberries.

6 egg whites, whipped
3 ounces confectioner's sugar
Defrost the raspberries if they are frozen.

1 8-ounce package raspberry gelatin (optional)

Place sponge cake in bottom of large glass, ovenproof bowl. Break it into pieces that fit — perfectly, of course. Measure them with a measuring tape so that each is where it is supposed to be. If you are recovering from perfectionism, throw the damn sponge wherever you want it to land in the bowl.

Pour the raspberries and accompanying juice onto the sponge so that it soaks in.

Whip up the egg whites until stiff and add some of the sugar. If the whites are really firm, you do not need the sugar but I prefer it.

Spread whipped egg whites over the mixture in the bowl and make sure the edges are covered.

Place in a 375° oven for about half an hour until the tips of the meringue (that's what you made with egg whites) are brown — light brown and cute looking.

Allow to cool and voila! Raspberry Surprise. If you cook like I do, the surprise may be what you left out.

Inner Child Carrot Cake

— Carla Wills-Brandon, M.A. —

Carla Wills-Brandon, M.A., is a national speaker and a therapist in private practice in Houston, Texas. Along with her husband, Michael, she works with families in recovery from addiction and abuse. She is the author of six books including: *Eat Like A Lady: A Guide To Recovery From Bulimia; Is It Love Or Is It Sex? Why Relationships Fail;* the best-selling *Learning To Say No: Establishing Healthy Boundaries; Where Do I Draw The Line? A Workbook For Establishing Healthy Boundaries* and *The Fourth Step: Reevaluating Our Childhood Survival Skills.* Together with Michael Brandon, Ph.D., she has authored *It's Not My Fault: A Child's Reader On Family Chemical Dependency.* Carla and Michael Brandon have been married for 14 years and have a five-year-old son named Aaron.

For years in adulthood I spent time resolving the many childhood family of origin issues which had kept me a prisoner from life as it was meant to be. Only after this was I able to look back and say "Not everything about childhood was bad." Along with the pain there was also some joy and fun. One of the family treasures I received while growing up was the ability to cook.

This love for cooking blossomed when I was about five years old, thanks to my Grandmother Wills. Her parents had migrated from Russia at the turn of the century and were of German descent. As a result of this, her house was always filled with the smell of home-made noodle soup, scratch-made meat pies, cakes of all kinds, cinnamon raisin stuffing with turkey, chicken or duck and hand-made German sausage. Going to Grandma Wills's house gave me a temporary escape from the craziness I was living with and most important, an opportunity to have some *fun*.

My Grandma taught me all of her cooking secrets and she also taught me about the joys of creative cooking. My first creative cooking venture was an apple pie made with peanut butter, and to this day I am still teased by my sister. Though I don't make plum pancakes or peanut butter apple pies anymore, if I'm stressed out or feeling overwhelmed with life, look out!

Today I cook to relax and unwind. If I've had a hard day, my husband Michael and son Aaron know the flour will fly, the egg beater will whirl, nuts will be chopped, the kitchen will be turned into a disaster area, but in the end, a delectable delight will be born. I continue to carry on my Grandmother's tradition of joyful cooking and can lose myself in creating a new taste.

My carrot cake was born in just this way. I was full of overwhelming feeling one day and needed a *feeling break*. I couldn't see things clearly and my perception was way off base. So to the kitchen I went. The result was a wonderful cake which was wheat free, often a concern for people with food allergies and addictions.

Making this cake encourages my creativity and provides me with opportunities to gather some serenity after a difficult day.

The next time life feels really unfair, or you're down and need a break from feeling blue, do what Grandma Wills taught me to do. Take a fun break and life will feel not quite as complicated as it did before.

Inner Child Carrot Cake

4 eggs
1 cup melted butter
2 cups sugar* or
    12 packets Sweet and Low*
1 teaspoon baking soda
2 teaspoons pumpkin pie spice
¼ teaspoon salt

1 16 oz. can cooked carrots
½ cup potato or corn starch
1½ cups rice flour
½ cup grated carrots
½ cup chopped walnuts
½ cup raisins

Beat together eggs, melted butter, sugar, baking soda, salt and pumpkin pie spice.

Mash cooked carrots and add to the above.

Separately, mix starch and rice flour together, then add to the above mixture.

Beat on low with electric mixer until smooth.

Add grated carrots, walnuts and raisins.

Pour into well-greased 9x13x4 glass baking pan.

Bake at 350° for 35-40 minutes or until cake bounces back and is firm on the top.

Cool for 10 minutes before removing from pan. Serve with vanilla frozen yogurt and enjoy your creation!

*See Healthy Substitutes, page 93.

Keep-It-Simple Cake

— Mitzi Chandler —

Mitzi Chandler is author of *Whiskey's Song; Gentle Reminders: Daily Affirmations For Co-Dependents; Lost And Found: A Story About Feelings* and *Late Bloomers: Weekly Inspiration For Women In Their Prime.*

This recipe was originally called Hobo Bread.
It could also be called Easy-Does-It Dessert.

Holidays are a hassle for most of us. There's too much of everything going on and we try to keep pace with it all. By the time Christmas or Hanukkah or a birthday arrives we may be exhausted and plumb out of good will. "Bah! Humbug!" may better express what we feel.

This cake is simple to make and is inexpensive. It is also sweet and delicious. It can be given as a gift or served up proudly to your guests. If you want something fancier and don't enjoy baking, let Sara Lee do it.

Keep-It-Simple Cake

1 cup water	2 teaspoons baking soda
1 cup sugar*	2 cups flour
2 tablespoons oil	1½ cup walnuts
1 egg	1½ cups raisins

To make this a spice cake add 1 teaspoon each:
cinnamon, nutmeg, cloves, allspice.

Boil raisins in the water for a few minutes, until they are plump.

Blend in sugar and oil.

Stir in egg, soda and flour.

Fold in nuts and spices.

Pour mixture into 3 or 4 greased and floured 16-ounce cans (the containers that are used for soups and veggies). Be sure to remove the paper labels.

Fill cans slightly more than half full.

Bake one hour at 325°.

Cool 15 minutes.

Slide cakes out of cans, relax and be done with it.

Wishing you an easy-does-it happy holiday. You deserve it.

*See Healthy Substitutions, page 93.

Grow Your Own Pumpkin Pie

— Diane Glynn —

Diane Glynn is president of Diane Glynn Publicity and Public Relations and has dedicated years of love and expertise to promoting the recovery movement. In private life she enjoys gardening, baking, long walks and country western dancing.

Grow Your Own Pumpkin Pie

This melts in your mouth and satisfies your soul, your tummy and your sweet tooth, all at once. No spices, just golden sweet. Perfect for a snack or dessert and wondrous cold out of the refrigerator for breakfast.

Start with a pumpkin grown in your garden, if possible. Watch the globe turn orange as the air turns crisp. Sweet sugar pumpkins are best for cooking. Or pick one up at the garden stand — not a big jack-o-lantern, but a smallish bright orange chubby ball with thick, smooth flesh.

There are lots of methods for cooking pumpkin, and I've tried most. I find the best is to cut it open, scoop out the seeds and slice it into chunks; pop it into a large pot to boil, skin and all. When a fork goes through, drain and slice off the skin. Then into a food mill for smooth, tasty pumpkin.

If all this is too much, store-bought cans of pumpkin will work; get unspiced, pure pumpkin, though.

Now for the pie . . .

THE CRUST

Prepare a pie crust — your recipe; just plain, regular pie crust. (Editor's Note: If you are a total klutz with pie crust and end up with dough of steel you have to chisel out of the pan, you don't have to keep setting yourself up for failure. Go to the store and buy prepared pretty good pie crust neatly frozen in its own pan and ready to receive the fabulous filling that follows.)

THE FILLING

2 cups mashed pumpkin
1 beaten egg
1 teaspoon melted butter

1 cup sugar*
½ teaspoon salt
1 teaspoon vanilla

½ cup canned evaporated milk

Mix all ingredients and pour into the unbaked pie crust.

Bake at 400° for 10 minutes. Then turn oven down to 325° for approximately 30 minutes more, or until a knife inserted in the pie comes out clean (like baking a custard). Don't overbake.

Serve this pie with whipped cream — lovely! But it's luxurious just plain, too.

*See Healthy Substitutions, page 93.

Spirithaven Baked Apple

— Sandy Bierig, M.Ed., C.A.C. —

Sandy Bierig, M.Ed., C.A.C., is author of *Transforming The Co-dependent Woman*. She was co-founder of *Serenity House,* and is presently in the process of developing *Spirithaven* on Cape Cod, Massachusetts, a safe space for women in recovery from the effects of alcoholism, addiction and co-dependence. She has four children and two grandchildren.

When she was growing up in post-depression Philadelphia, food was hearty but plain, and treats were in short supply so they meant a lot. Among her most memorable were the sundae at the local drugstore counter, and the chocolate milkshake on the way to have her tonsils removed.

Today, Sandy says she would rather eat and do the dishes and let someone else cook, but she is still always right on time when dinner is ready.

Anyone who really knows me would have been able to predict that my contribution to this book would involve desserts. It's no understatement to say that I love sweets. I would rather eat them, in any form, than anything else I can imagine. However, I try to balance my eating today, so I have been forced to find adequate substitutes for the cakes and ice cream and cookies that I used to crave.

My search has led me back to the very things that my mother used to insist I eat as a child — fruit. I can eat it cold, feeling like a kid again while trying not to dribble its juices down my arms and on my clothes. I can serve it with relative formality, with a sprinkle of granola and a dollop of frozen yogurt. I can cook it, bake it or nuke it (and I don't remove edible skins because that's where a lot of vitamins are stored). Sometimes I combine different kinds of fruit, cook it a little and I have a compote. Or I stir it together with some sugar-free whipped cream substitute and I have ambrosia straight from Mount Olympus.

Nowadays the supermarkets carry lots of exotic fruits from all over the world. So if you're watching your weight or changing your eating habits for the better, don't go all rigid and decide that you need to cut out sweets altogether. Pick a fruit — any fruit — and enjoy!

The recipe for baked apple that follows is one that is close to my heart as well as my stomach. It is an autonomous sweet (that is to say, a single portion) for the weight- and health-conscious who would rather just indulge, but are unwilling to bulge more than necessary. I use it to nurture myself — safely and occasionally to nurture other people. That's why I call it "Spirithaven."

Spirithaven Baked Apple

1 medium to large apple (my personal favorite is a red delicious)
2 tablespoons water

¼ teaspoon low-fat margarine
1 tablespoon raisins
A sprinkle of granola

Cinnamon to taste (lots for me)

Core apple, cut in half, leaving skin on.

Put water, margarine, raisins and granola in a small microwave-safe bowl.

Place apple face down on these ingredients and sprinkle liberally with cinnamon.

Cover loosely with wax paper and cook in microwave on high for about 6 minutes, or until apple is soft. (Non-nukers can cover and bake in 350° oven for 20 minutes to half an hour.)

When apple is done, put it in a bowl, skin side down, and pour the raisin and granola sauce all over it.

Cut it into bite-size pieces and add frozen yogurt or light-style whipped cream substitute according to your conscience.

(*Editor's Note:* Or bypass your conscience and go ahead and use *real* whipped cream.)

Reliving Baked Alaska

— Anne Zevin, M.A. —

Anne Zevin, M.A., is a family therapist with a private practice in Cataumet, Massachusetts. She is co-author of *When A Family Needs Therapy*.

I grew up in the depression in a Yankee family where food was not discussed. Married in 1951, I had no notion of how to cook. An adventuress in life, so was I in the kitchen.

I remember the stunning arrivals of garlic, olive oil, sour cream, thyme and red caviar into my life. I dimly understood there was something I didn't know. And so I set about Knowing.

I was determined to become sophisticated. Actually I was determined to become more sophisticated than my mother. I drove myself to more and more fabulous heights, spurning anything reminiscent of my mother's jellied salad molds and date nut bars. I looked down my nose at her Hawaiian chicken with pineapple rings and produced coq au vin with a reduced sauce. If she made scalloped potatoes with grated cheese, I did rice pilaf with chestnuts and oysters. I was riding for a fall.

Reliving Baked Alaska

I no longer remember where I encountered my first baked Alaska, but I offered to make it for Easter dinner, replacing my mother's angel cake with strawberry sauce and vanilla ice cream.

The day arrived. I arrived in the kitchen with all the ingredients. My 85-year-old grandfather, a Maine dairy and chicken farmer, stayed in his chair in the kitchen and watched with what I knew to be awe.

I laid out the sponge cake (which I had made from scratch) on the baking sheet and put the rectangular block of Hood's ice cream in the ice tray compartment of the refrigerator.

Here's Irma Rombauer's recipe for the meringue:

6 egg whites
6 tablespoons confectioner's sugar
A pinch of salt

¼ teaspoon arrowroot
or cream of tartar
1 teaspoon vanilla

I separated the eggs very carefully and beat the whites in my mother's new Mixmaster, folding in the sugar, salt, arrowroot and vanilla.

I preheated the oven to 450°. We ate dinner — roast lamb, of course (overdone). As others cleared, I went back to my post in the kitchen. Gramp followed and reclaimed his chair.

I quickly put the ice cream on the sponge cake, leaving a 1-inch edge of cake sticking out all around, and slathered the egg whites, which were a bit soggy by now, all over the ice cream, being careful not to leave spaces, and explained to Gramp that the egg whites were insulation.

I then popped it all into the oven and told the family and guests there would be a twenty-five minute wait.

Twenty minutes later, I went back to the oven to check. Gramp followed. We opened the door to behold a half-gallon of Hood's vanilla ice cream running all over the bottom of the oven through the broiler pan and out onto the floor.

I began a flurry of, "I can't imagine what happened . . ." Gramp straightened up and said: "Any damn fool knows you can't cook ice cream in the oven."

Forty years have gone by. I have become somewhat more humble. I managed to produce a baked Alaska intact after I realized that the insulating egg whites needed to be freshly beaten and stiff and that I had to check the oven every five minutes as the meringue was browning.

Only once since then have I seen baked Alaska, and that was served in 1973 in a famous restaurant with the whole roast pig feast in Toledo, Spain, to a crowd of rowdy Americans who stood on the table and sang the Star Spangled Banner at the huge baked Alaska flambé.

No, I never learned to flambé it, but I wish Gramp had been there.

Junkfood Communication

— Deborah M. Hazelton, Ed.S., M.A. —

Deborah M. Hazelton, Ed.S., M.A., is author of *Solving The Self-Esteem Puzzle* and *The Courage To See: Daily Affirmations For Healing The Shame Within.* A licensed mental health counselor, she is also an ordained minister and a national consultant and speaker on issues of adult children, abuse and people who live with disabilities. She is president and founder of InnerSight Unlimited in Deerfield Beach, Florida, where she resides with her working guide dog, Lyndi.

Junkfood Communication

The old saying has it that, "You are what you eat." Those who aspire to health foods or special diets would contend that this is true.

I will add that, "You are also what you say and what you swallow."

So what verbal messages are you dishing out these days? Are they deep fried, coated in so much floury surface that the person who swallows them doesn't even know what it was they ate and got indigestion later? Do you dish out words you often eat later as they repeat and repeat in your mind — like putdowns, criticism, gossip or lies? Do you coat messages with so much sugar that the person gets a high and a crashing letdown when the sugar wears off?

And what about all the junkfood communication you swallow? How about all the messages you get where your boundaries are not respected, where decisions are made for you? How about assumptions, expectations and caustic humorous remarks? Do you swallow them? It's hard to digest much of anything after that. The stuff just sits there and then you might wonder why you have interpersonal indigestion. Heartburn? Oh, that poor heart! It gets burned in some of those relationships, doesn't it?

Do you eat to comfort old feelings or crave enough love to fill old hunger?

Fill up with healthy verbal thoughts for food and you'll dish out messages you can feel whole and healthy about. Messages of kindness, support, honest constructive opinions and even silence.

Resolve to fill your appetite with only healthy thought for food, so that the messages you swallow are nourishing to your spirit, your emotions and your body. You can directly let some people know that you're not going to accept verbal abuse — or, as the 12-Step programs say, you can "Take what you like and leave the rest."

So, unless you want to go on an occasional verbal junkfood binge, watch those deep-fried feelings and that interpersonal indigestion. Don't be weighed down or constantly hungry from the effects of junkfood communication.

Lovefood

— Valerie Wells —

As a visualization consultant, Valerie Wells has developed personalized mental imagery to help clients eliminate negative images and replace them with positive images of success.

Her fast, fun, motivational visualizations air daily on South Florida radio station WWNN and an audiocassette of ten visualizations is also available. Her motivational seminars, "Envisioneering," have been presented to both professional and lay groups.

She is the author of *The Joy Of Visualization*. Her articles have appeared in such newspapers as the *Boston Globe, Chicago Tribune, Los Angeles Times* and *Miami Herald,* and in magazines such as *Self, South Florida* and *New Miami.*

Lovefood

A VISUALIZATION FOR HEART AND MIND

What have you been feeding your heart and mind? Leftover feelings? Stale ideas? Frozen frustration? Half-baked dreams? If you're hungry for something fresh and nourishing, here's a recipe for hearty love food.

First decide where you want to enjoy your love meal, creating a mental image, or sense, of the environment. Do you want to eat at home, in a restaurant or some special spot outdoors? What size and shape is the table? Does it have placemats or a tablecloth? Candles? Flowers? What design is the chair?

What does the place setting look like? Are you going to use silverware or goldware? What color is the plate? Is it china or ceramic? Does it have a design on it? Maybe good luck symbols are scattered across it, or your initials are intertwined with hearts, or flowers, or stars. Around the rim of the plate, written in gaily colored letters, see your positive slogan: "I am nourished by love." Or, "I am filled with love and light." Or, "Love energizes me."

Now picture, or sense, your stove. On the burners are pots and pans in which love food is cooking. The pots have lids on them, but the aromas that escape and curl into your nostrils are tantalizing. Something is baking in the oven and smells delicious.

Who's doing the cooking? It might be you or someone else. It could be someone you know: mother, father, friend, lovemate. Or it could be someone you don't know: your fairy godmother, Wolfgang Puck, Mary Poppins or Winnie-the-Pooh. Create whomever you want to cook love food for you. Let there be one cook or several, each one contributing their specialty.

Take your plate, the one with your personal slogan around the rim, and holding it in one hand or setting it down next to the stove, begin to serve yourself your love meal. Lift the lid of the pan nearest to you. Inside is love. Does it simmer or sizzle? What color is love? What shape? Help yourself to a big hunk. If you're really hungry, take two or three pieces — you can have as much love as you want. Put a generous serving on your plate.

Lifting the lid on the next pot, you discover optimism. Optimism might look like fresh yellow corn, or maybe new green peas. Spoon a heaping portion onto your plate next to the love.

In the third pot vitality tea is bubbling briskly. It is clear like light? Golden like honey? Red like a hibiscus flower? Pour it into the cup or mug that matches your plate.

Baking in the oven is enthusiasm bread. Cut yourself a thick slice. Is it white bread or whole grain? Does it have nuts, or maybe heart-shaped raisins? Put the bread on your plate.

Is there anything else you need or want to make your love meal complete? A sauce of light for the love, perhaps? A dollop of open-minded jam for the bread? A vivacious condiment? A spoonful of elation to sweeten the tea?

Carry your full plate and brimming cup to the place you have chosen and set them down on the table. Sit down and enjoy your love meal. This can be a special dinner just for you, or you can invite someone to share your love with — you can even throw a dinner party.

The love is so tender you can cut it with your fork. It's warm and smooth in your mouth and seems to melt. What flavor is love? Taste some optimism. Drink some vitality. Take a few bites of enthusiasm.

Love food nourishes feelings, freshens ideas and enriches dreams. You can eat all the love food you want, whenever you want. It's non-fattening and it nourishes the good feelings you have for yourself.

Recipe For Pot Luck

— A Final Word from the Editor —

Start with an idea,
a desire, a need, a hunger.
A purpose for getting people together.

Do the best with what you have.
Invite others to bring
the best of what they have.
Go ahead and share your dreams.

Before you know it
there's more than enough
for everybody.

Essential ingredients:
enthusiasm
a liberal dash of good humor
openness to surprise.

Healthy Substitutions

Sugar

In most recipes that call for sugar, you can substitute raw, unadulterated honey, thereby employing some bees and adding some food value in the form of minerals. *The Joy Of Cooking* says for each cup of sugar in a recipe you can use 1 cup of honey and leave out ¼ cup of liquid. If you're trying to wean yourself from sweets, try cutting the amount of honey in half.

Beware of artificial sweeteners. The chemicals in them may be worse for you than sugar.

Salt

If you are on a salt-restricted diet and bland food makes you suffer, know that there are other things you can use to bring out the taste. Fresh lemon juice adds tanginess to salad dressings, soups, fish and chicken. Herbs like thyme, marjoram and rosemary will jazz up almost any dish you make. For a hot kick try tabasco or cilantro.

Food Allergies

If you are allergic to dairy products, eggs, fermented foods, flour, sugar, caffeine, the nightshade family of vegetables or anything else you find yummy, you don't have to go through the rest of your life feeling deprived. Browse among the books and products in your health food store until you familiarize yourself with new ways of eating. Like any other form of recovery, changing your food habits takes awareness and work, but both your body and soul will flourish as a result.